Russell Westbrook

The Inspirational Story of Basketball Superstar Russell Westbrook

presentation of the information is without contract or any type of guarantee assurance.

The trademarks that are used are without any consent, and the publication of the trademark is without permission or backing by the trademark owner. All trademarks and brands within this book are for clarifying purposes only and are the owned by the owners themselves, not affiliated with this document.

Table Of Contents

Introduction

As the title already implies, this is a short book about [The Inspirational Story of Basketball Superstar Russell Westbrook] and how he rose from his life in Los Angeles, California to become one of today's leading and most-respected basketball players. In his rise to superstardom, Russell has inspired not only the youth, but fans of all ages throughout the world.

This book also portrays the struggles that Russell has had to overcome during his early childhood years, his teen years, and up until he became who he is today. A notable source of inspiration is Russell's service to the community and his strong connection with the fans of the sport. He continues to serve as a polarizing, fun-loving superstar in a sport that glorifies flashy plays and mega personalities.

Combining a deadly pull-up jump shot, incredible athleticism, a ferocious attacking style, and high basketball IQ, Russell has shown the ability to completely take over a game. From being a young undersized teen to becoming one of the greatest guards of his generation, you'll learn here how this man has risen to the ranks of the best basketball players today.

Thanks again for grabbing this book. Hopefully you can take some of the examples and lessons from Russell's story and apply them to your own life!

Chapter 1:

Youth & Family Life

Russell Westbrook Jr. was born on November 12th, 1988 in Long Beach, California. His father, Russell Westbrook Sr., and mother, Shannon Horton, welcomed him as their first of two sons. Russell would grow up in Hawthorne, California and would become infatuated with the sport of basketball, just like many young males in the Southern California area.

But it was not all basketball and games for the Westbrook children. Their mom Shannon made sure that studies were the top priority of the household. Russell was in fact among the top students in his class, as he was an honor student. His favorite subject? Math.

When it came to basketball, Russell Sr. took the reigns. During his youth, Russell Jr. was mentored by his father. He learned the proper fundamentals of the game from his old man. Their favorite place to play ball would be at Ross Snyder Park in the neighborhood of Compton. As soon as Russell was old enough to be out and about, he would follow his father to the court and watch him play in pick-up games. As Russell Sr. would showcase his moves in between the white lines, Russell Jr. would be on the sidelines copying them as best he could.

As his father noticed Russell's obvious interest in the sport, he would go on to coach him along as best he could. The two would go through daily drills and even discuss basketball strategies that were proven to be effective.

Russell would go on to attend Leuzinger High School in Lawndale and had desires to play for the varsity squad as soon as possible. Despite his impressive physical frame that you see today, Russell was not always the most imposing or most athletic guy on the court. In fact, as a freshman at Leuzinger High, Russell only stood at 5 foot 9 inches and weighed 140 pounds. Despite his small stature for a ball player, Russell wore a size 14 shoe, a sign that he might have a growth spurt in him.

Because of this size disadvantage, Russell was not able to see significant playing time for the team until his senior year. He did not even crack his team's starting line-up until his junior year of high school. However, after hitting a growth spurt of five inches, Russell blossomed into a star guard that the team could rely on in clutch moments.

His impressive statistics consisted of over 25 points and almost 9 rebounds per game, to go along with 2 assists and 3 steals. His season high would be a 51 point explosion that was locally talked about for a long time. It was evident even at this young age, Russell could rebound extremely well for the guard position. Not only were his collective season statistics impressive, but Russell was also able to post fourteen double-doubles and score over thirty points in eight different games.

Most importantly, Russell was able to lead the school to a 25-4 record and they made the quarterfinals in the state playoffs. Because of his impressive individual season and the team's success, Russell drew some local and even some national attention. He would eventually go on to earn First-Team All-CIF honors and was even listed as a Top 25 guard in the nation by Scout.com.

A significant event during Russell's childhood was the death of close friend, Khelcey Barrs. Khelcey was a supremely talented player on Russell's high school team. Arguably with even more potential than Russell, Khelcey was being tracked down by major college basketball programs as a high school sophomore. Not only was his talent at an elite level, but his frame of 6'6" and 200 pounds as a sophomore showed that he had the physical tools as well.

Unfortunately during a late night pick-up game on the court, Khelcey died from cardiomegaly, an abnormal enlargement of the heart. It was a tragic event that nobody saw coming. This loss would affect Russell's attitude and he would never forget his close friend. Even to this day, Russell wears a wristband that reads "KB3" on it. Khelcey's basketball number was 3 and his legacy will live on as long as people like Russell carry it into the mainstream light.

Russell would not let this negatively impact his drive, rather he learned to harness the emotions he felt from Khelcey's death and played with even more ferocity on the court. His aggressive play became evident and defenders were at his mercy once he decided to attack them with his downhill charging style.

During Russell's youth, he became a fan of Earvin "Magic" Johnson, the legendary point guard and star of the hometown Los Angeles Lakers. Even though Russell did not grow up in the era of Magic's prime, he enjoyed watching his games. He admired Magic's playing style and effectiveness as a floor general. Russell Sr. would show his son old films of Magic and the Lakers, then the elder Westbrook would break down Johnson's moves.

An interesting aside about Russell's youth is that he was not able to dunk the basketball until the end of his senior year of high school. He had always possessed the natural athleticism but was not able to use it to his advantage, until his growth spurt combined with the hard work that he put in during the offseason. This is almost unbelievable to many people who have become fans of Russell as a professional, because these days he is considered to be the most explosive point guard to ever play the game.

Even with all those God-given gifts on the basketball court and the statistics to back it up, Russell wasn't heavily recruited out of high school. In fact, 247Sports only considered him a 3-star prospect. The leading recruiting website placed Russell at #151 in the national ranking and #36 at the shooting guard position. He was also only the 17th best prospect out of the state of California. He was, however, included in *Long Beach Press-Telegram*'s Best in the West Third Team, while also earning All-State honors.

Russell's potential would not go completely unnoticed, as coach Ben Howland of UCLA would offer him an athletic scholarship to play for the school's basketball program. As Jordan Farmar and a few other players would be leaving the school, there would be a need for another guard to play on the squad.

Russell watched a lot of UCLA games during his high school years. Like any other youngster in the neighborhood that picked up a basketball, he was a big fan of the Bruins and their exciting play style. He had always dreamt of playing for his favorite school, but things didn't pan out immediately for Russell. While Howland showed some interest, he didn't immediately offer him a scholarship.

The decision of their starting guards – Jordan Farmar and Arron Afflalo – regarding whether to apply for the NBA Draft or stay in school was part of the reason why UCLA was hesitant about drafting Russell. However, according to Larry Harris, a former Arizona State assistant coach under Herb Sendek, Howland was looking at another kid in the area – another guard. Harris believed this is why they didn't lock Russell up early. Initially, this was a big turnoff for the young player.

The Sun Devils coaching staff took this as a sign and swooped in to court Russell. Arizona State recently snatched Herb Sendek from North Carolina State as replacement for the fired Rob Evans. Sendek quickly went to work by scouting Russell. Sendek, who signed rather late (April) into the offseason, remembers thinking of recruiting whoever was left among the top unsigned high school players, and Russell was one of them.

Sendek and his staff visited Russell and watched him play. Russell agreed to meet with Sendek mainly because of the latter's reputation for developing players. In addition, Russell knew his game still had a long ways to go. They invited him to campus, but since it was an unofficial visit, Russell had to drive himself all the way to Arizona. The Sun Devils hoped the long travel wouldn't scare him away. Nevertheless, it didn't really matter in the end; Russell's heart was fixed on the Bruins.

After the ASU visit, UCLA came calling and finally offered Russell a scholarship. It was actually assistant coach Kerry Keating's call. He had loved Russell since he saw him play a couple of years prior. He convinced Howland to take a chance on the kid, which the coach finally did. Russell committed to UCLA on April 19th, 2006.

It's ironic to note that the Sun Devils, after missing out on Russell, later signed another future NBA All-Star to a letter of intent shortly after the 2006 NCAA season started, James Harden. One can only imagine what an ASU backcourt of Westbrook and Harden could have done in the college scene.

Before UCLA got a hold of Russell, he was the one knocking on the doors of a number of schools hoping to get a scholarship and a spot on their varsity team. Before his senior year in high school, Russell attended an elite camp by former Chicago Bulls coach Tim Floyd, who was then coaching the University of Southern California. Back then, the USC coaches were undecided about Russell's potential. They saw him as a classic tweener; he was not tall enough to play shooting guard, but his play style was not that of a true point guard. Since the Trojans needed a point guard badly, they passed on Russell.

By the end, UCLA and Arizona State were not the only schools that checked out Russell. Since he hailed from Southern California, most of the Pacific-10 teams scouted him. Other schools from different conferences also saw something in him. Those who offered him scholarships were Miami (FL), San Diego, Boston College, Wake Forest, and Washington showed interest but didn't tender an offer.

For a while, many believed Kent State had the inside track on the future NBA All-Star. A former assistant coach, Josh Oppenheimer, was close friends with Russell's high school coach. That connection paved the way for Kent State to scout Russell early on. The first time they saw him play, they immediately loved him and started recruiting him. During Russell's visit to the school, the young baller was impressed. Russell also toured Creighton's campus a week before visiting Kent State. They were the only two schools that got official visits from Russell.

Chapter 2:

College Years

Russell had much to prove as he entered the University of California-Los Angeles. He was not heavily recruited out of high school and according to many, Coach Howland had taken a shot with him. His recruiting class wasn't at par with previous classes as the only ranked recruit aside from Russell was forward James Keefe of California. Russell decided to go with the number "0" for his college career and entered the season as a wild-card for the team.

Despite what was perceived by many as a sub-par recruiting class, the 2006-07 UCLA basketball roster was about as loaded as you would find in college basketball during Russell's time there. Even with Jordan Farmar gone to the NBA, the team was stacked at the guard position. In his first season, Russell would come off the bench behind All Pac-10 First Team point guard, Darren Collison, and Pac-10 Player of the Year, Arron Afflalo.

This three guard combination was considered to be one of the best in the entire country and Russell gained a reputation as a defensive specialist, even if he played a mere nine minutes per game. In his limited playing time, Russell was able to average just over three points and almost an assist per game. It's quite hard to believe that his career high in points during his freshman season was just 11, which he did twice, considering he would become one of the best NBA scorers in recent memory.

The team was able to advance to the Final Four in the NCAA Tournament but was not able to get any further. For the season, Russell was certainly a productive player for the team but would not receive any accolades from the outside, as his playing time was not substantial. He would spend quite a bit of time on the bench during the NCAA Tournament.

This lack of opportunity on the court would become a blessing in disguise for Russell, as he leveraged his emotions into motivation to become even better. His offseason was spent with many hours in the gym, spending long days improving all aspects of his game. His family would motivate him and believe in his abilities and he sought a bigger role going into his sophomore year.

Russell' efforts paid off, as he was able to score 12.7 points per game to go along with 4.3 assists,

3.9 rebounds and 1.6 steals, as well as cementing his reputation as a defensive stopper on the perimeter. In many games, Russell would be assigned to guard the opposing team's best perimeter scorer.

Furthermore, Russell was also able to play a significant role in UCLA's Final Four appearance. He scored 22 points to lead the Bruins in their losing effort against the Memphis Tigers. Russell added 3 rebounds and two assists and steals each, while Kevin Love and Luc Richard Mbah a Moute chipped in 12 points each.

The Tigers were led by one-and-done freshman sensation Derrick Rose (25 points, 9 rebounds and 4 assists) and fellow future NBA draftees Chris Douglas-Roberts (28 points), and Joey Dorsey (0 points, 15 rebounds). C-USA Tournament MVP Antonio Anderson added 12 points for the winning side. Despite the disappointing end to the season, Russell would be recognized for his efforts as he was named the Pac-10 Defensive Player of the Year as well as given Third Team All Pac-10 honors.

Russell's sophomore season also allowed him to develop a relationship with new big man, Kevin Love. The two phenoms were roommates during the season and developed a friendship both on and off the court. They also complimented each other's playing style, as Kevin was a very skilled big man who would benefit off of Russell's penetration. Also, Kevin's ability to snag anything around the rim and fire long, precise outlet passes allowed Russell and the other guards to get easy buckets in transition. The team would consist of Westbrook, Collison, Love, and Mbah a Moute, all players who would have solid careers in the NBA. Providing support were starting wingman Josh Shipp and reserves Lorenzo Mata-Real, Alfred Aboya, and James Keefe.

In his sophomore campaign, Russell also showed his explosive abilities when he made a number of highlight plays above the rim. His powerful dunks and acrobatic lay-ups made him a fan favorite and kept spectators on their feet. Upon season's end, Russell used the momentum of his sophomore season and decided that he would be best served to enter the upcoming NBA Draft.

As a prospect, Russell was considered raw and there was debate about whether or not he could play the point guard position. Because he had played the off-guard position for much of his UCLA career, he was not seen as a "traditional" point guard, rather as a hybrid guard.

Many "experts" and scouts around the league, figured that Russell was not worth the risk because he had high potential as a bust and did not have star potential at the highest level. There were even some who felt that Russell would be better served to stay in school rather than to attempt a career in the NBA. Nonetheless, there were some people up in Seattle that felt Russell could be much more, and with the fourth pick in the 2008 NBA Draft, the Seattle SuperSonics drafted Russell to be their point guard of the future.

Chapter 3:

Professional Life

First Season (2008-09)

After Russell was chosen number four overall behind Derrick Rose, Michael Beasley, and O. J. Mayo, there were many questions about how he would fit in with the team - mainly from outside of the organization. The franchise would soon move from Seattle to Oklahoma City and become the Oklahoma City Thunder, due to the team's sale and relocation. By early July, Russell and the Thunder had agreed to a contract.

Russell quickly proved his doubters wrong, as he started the season off with a bang. He worked well alongside rising star, Kevin Durant, to develop chemistry on the rebuilding team. The team's fans turned into one of the loudest fanbases in the entire league by the end of the season and Russell's status as a rising star would not be a question by year's end.

He posted a triple double in his first year, becoming the first rookie since Chris Paul to accomplish such a feat in a rookie season. He posted averages of over 15.3 points, 5.3 assists, 4.9 rebounds and 1.3 steals per game in his first season. The Thunder rookie finished fourth in the NBA Rookie of the Year voting behind Rose, Mayo, and Brook Lopez. He was also recognized as a member of the NBA's All-Rookie First Team.

Second Season (2009-10)

Russell entered his second season as the team's starting point guard and showed noticeable improvement as the team's ball-handler. His decision-making abilities and pull-up jump shot greatly improved over the off-season and he would go on to have some stellar individual performances. He would post averages of sixteen points per game, eight assists, five rebounds and almost one and a half steals per game. He also recorded a career-high 16 assists in a game against Minnesota. While his numbers showed that he could be an all-around player at this level, they didn't show all the aspects of his game. He was already considered a brilliant defensive player and his hustle was incomparable.

With the help of newcomers James Harden and Serge Ibaka, the Oklahoma City Thunder were beginning to build a talented, youthful core. This reflected itself in the team's record, as they were able to more than double their win total from the previous year to 50 wins for the season. Surprising to most around the league, the Thunder would end up making the Playoffs as the eighth seed in the loaded Western Conference.

In the first round, the Thunder would meet the dominant Los Angeles Lakers, but were able to play them very tough and even threatened to win the series. However, the Los Angeles Lakers were able to close them out and go on to win the NBA Finals that same year. Personally, Russell was able to step his game up in the postseason, something that would become a trend in his career. He averaged over twenty points, six rebounds, and six assists a game against the Lakers, to go along with over three steals per game.

The year served as a sign that there were bright times ahead in Oklahoma City. Very few people outside of the organization took the team seriously before Russell's second year, but things were about to change.

Another bright sign for Russell was being named to the United States Men's Basketball Team that would play against some of the world's best in the 2010 FIBA World Championship. The so-called "B Team" was a complete departure from the 2008 Olympic team popularly known as the Redeem Team featuring Kobe Bryant, LeBron James, Carmelo Anthony, Dwyane Wade, Dwight Howard, Chris Paul, and Jason Kidd.

Among Russell's teammates on the 2010 USA team were Kevin Durant, Derrick Rose, Stephen Curry, Kevin Love, Chauncey Billups, Rudy Gay,

Andre Iguodala, Danny Granger, Eric Gordon, Lamar Odom and Tyson Chandler. They continued the US redemption in the sport by winning the gold over a Turkish team led by Hedo Turkoglu and Ersan Ilyasova. Russell's six assists led the team in their game against Angola during the Round of 16. The FIBA Worlds win also helped USA regain its Number 1 world ranking, which was previously held by Argentina thanks to its surprising win in the 2004 Olympics.

Third Season (2010-11)

Russell would use his third season to make the jump from a young starting point guard with potential, to a dominant force that could become a perennial All-Star. By the end of November, Russell had already posted a 43 point game against the Indiana Pacers. Within a week of that performance, he would go on to score 38 points, grab 15 rebounds, and dish out 9 assists in a game against the New Jersey Nets. His 15 rebounds were a then career-high and rare for someone his size. He would go on to become a triple-double machine as his career progressed. In fact, Russell has 42 career triple-doubles as of the 2015-16 NBA season. Thirty-seven of those came during the regular season, which is the seventh most in NBA history.

These types of performances put Russell on the map amongst fans and coaches. So much so, that he would be named to the 2011 NBA All-Star Game for the Western Conference. It was his first All-Star appearance and he was able to play alongside star teammate Kevin Durant in the game. The two were beginning to form one of the best young duos in the entire league.

By season's end, Russell's statistics showed a big jump as he improved in pretty much every single statistical category. His scoring average of almost 22 points per game put him among the top scoring guards in the game. His average of more than eight assists and almost five rebounds and two steals per game really showed that his all-around abilities were truly special. To top off his impressive season, Russell would also be named to the All-NBA Second Team.

The Thunder would take another jump as a team, finishing with 55 wins for the season and made it to the second round of the Playoffs to play the Dallas Mavericks. However, Dallas was just too determined, as Dirk Nowitzki and company went on a memorable run to win the NBA Championship. This would be the second year in a row that the Thunder would lose to the eventual Finals champions. Russell showed that he thrived in clutch moments once again, as he scored almost 24 points a game in the Playoffs and was able to create many scoring opportunities for his teammates.

Fourth Season (2011-12)

Russell would use the momentum from his impressive 2010-11 campaign to improve as an overall player once again. A notable performance included his 45 point game against former college roommate and still friend, Kevin Love, and his Minnesota Timberwolves. For the regular season, Russell was able to keep his statistics right up to par with his previous season, but showed a noticeable improvement in his ability to make plays for others.

He was becoming a much better on-court leader for the team and showed confidence and trust in his teammates. He would go on to make his second Western Conference All-Star Game appearance and would be named to the All-NBA Second Team for the second straight year.

Despite a lockout-shortened NBA season, the Thunder were able to keep their groove and play an impressive regular season. They moved through the Western Conference Playoffs, beating the Mavericks, Grizzlies, and Spurs. After such impressive series performances, the trio of Durant, Westbrook, and Harden were in the national spotlight.

The Thunder would meet the Miami Heat in the 2012 NBA Finals. While the main attraction of the Finals were the high-scoring rivals LeBron James and Kevin Durant, Russell posted some great performances that stole the show. His brilliant play catapulted himself into the conversation for best point guards in the league. He would score 27 points and dish out 11 assists in a Game 1 victory, joining Michael Jordan as the only player to put up 25+ points and 10+ assists in their Finals debut. Also, in a Game 4 defeat, Russell would score a playoff career high of 43 points.

Unfortunately, the Thunder would lose to the Heat in five games and face another off-season with mixed emotions. They were obviously ahead of schedule compared to most rebuilding situations but they also wanted to win a championship so badly, and were given the chance that year - only to come up short.

A sort of consolation came his way later that summer. Russell was chosen to represent the United States at the 2012 London Olympics. As expected, the USA Team was a collection of basketball superstars. Russell shared the court with current and former teammates Durant, Love, and Harden along with LeBron James, Kobe Bryant, Carmelo Anthony, Chris Paul, Tyson Chandler, Andre Iguodala and Deron Williams.

Blake Griffin was also selected but incurred an injury forcing him to give up his spot in favor of NBA rookie and number one draft pick Anthony Davis. Being chosen to play for his country was indeed a great honor and Russell returned the favor by helping the team bring home gold. Russell averaged 8.5 points in eight games. He had a team high 9 assists during their game against Great Britain.

Fifth Season (2012-13)

Russell and the Thunder would enter the season determined to make another run deep into the playoffs, even with the loss of James Harden to the Houston Rockets. Russell would make the NBA All-Star Game once again and his leadership continued to improve. By this point, Russell's pull-up jump shot was one of the most feared in the league, keeping defenders on their heels. Not only could Russell blow by a defender at will, but he could pull up and drain a jumper in a defender's face, leaving them to pick their poison in a 1-on-1 matchup.

The team was able to earn the number one seed in the Western Conference Playoffs and were considered by many as a favorite to win the NBA Finals. However, during the second game of the first round, Russell was hit on the knee by opposing point guard Patrick Beverley in controversial fashion.

Beverley was attempting to steal the ball from Russell as he was calling time-out and instead ran into Russell's knee in an awkward collision. Russell would continue the game in pain and finished with 29 points, giving the Thunder a 2-0 series lead. However, after further evaluation the next day, it was determined that Russell had suffered a tear in his right meniscus.

Seen as too risky to play with, Russell was conclusively told to shut his season down and go under the knife for surgery. This would result in him missing the rest of the Playoffs and took a huge slash into the Thunder's ability to be considered as serious contenders. The team would be able to use the 2-0 series lead to get by the Rockets but did not advance past their second round match-up with the Memphis Grizzlies.

Despite the controversy surrounding the injury, Russell ended the season with optimism and sat in the stands cheering on his team while being on crutches. He would go on to be named to the All-NBA Second Team for the third consecutive year and cement his place as a superstar in the league.

Sixth Season (2013-14)

Russell would undergo a second surgery on his right knee during the off-season, forcing him to set his return date to two weeks into the regular season. However, Russell was able to surprise the league by returning after only the first two games - feeding into his super-human persona that fans love about him.

Russell was back in true form before long and even posted a triple double in only a little over two quarters against the New York Knicks on Christmas Day. Surprisingly, after this incredible performance, there was an announcement that Russell would need to undergo arthroscopic surgery on his right knee once again. The injury would force him out until the All-Star break, ending his streak of consecutive All-Star appearances.

However, the team was able to develop in ways that it would not have imagined, as players like Reggie Jackson, Steven Adams, and most notably Kevin Durant, were able to take on bigger roles and expand their games. After Russell's return, the coaching staff made sure to handle him with caution, as he played the remainder of the season under a minute restriction. He would also sit out on the second night of back-to-backs, allowing him even more rest.

However, even under this restriction, Russell was able to record his second triple double of the season in just twenty minutes - the second fastest triple-double in NBA history. The team would finish with the second seed after winning almost sixty games for the season. They would make it to the Conference Finals where they played the San Antonio Spurs. However, this time around they had their two star offensive players but lacked their defensive anchor in the middle in Serge Ibaka.

After the Spurs dominated the paint in the first two games, Serge would return and give a valiant effort to protect the paint and hit his mid-range jumpers. However, it was too little too late for the Thunder, as the Spurs were able to close them out in six games.

Russell would find himself in the record books alongside Michael Jordan once again, when he scored forty points, dished out ten assists, grabbed five rebounds, and stole the ball five times. Russell and "His Airness" were the only players to ever do this in a playoff game.

For the entirety of the postseason, Russell would post historical statistics, with an average of almost 27 points per game, eights assists per game, and seven rebounds per game. He was the first player to average these numbers since Oscar Robertson, who did it half a century earlier.

This elevation in Russell's impact was felt in each round of the playoffs, as he was often assigned to lock down the opposing team's best guard while providing offensive brilliance at the same time. Not only that, but Russell emerged as the undisputed best rebounding point guard in the league. Even Clippers coach Doc Rivers was in awe of Russell's rebounding abilities when he faced their team.

For the season, the superstar guard played in just 46 games, the lowest so far in his career. He still managed to score in the 20s with a 21.8 PPG average to go with 5.7 rebounds, 6.9 assists and 1.9 steals per game.

Seventh Season (2014-15)

With Kevin Durant starting the 2014-15 campaign on the sideline, Russell was forced to take over for the franchise player, and he opened the season with guns blazing. He torched the Portland Trailblazers with 38 points, though the team failed to get the win. Unfortunately, it would take some time before Russell could score that much again. In fact, Russell had to wait until the end of November before he could suit up again for the Thunder.

He missed 14 consecutive games because of a hand injury he sustained during the team's second game (vs. the Clippers) of the season. The fiery guard injured his shooting hand during the second quarter, but still played on. He was later evaluated and discovered to have incurred a second metacarpal injury.

With Westbrook and Durant out, the team only managed to get four wins while racking up twelve losses. In his first game back, Russell didn't show any lingering effects of the injury. He scored 32 points to lift the Thunder over the New York Knicks.

The Thunder All-Star incurred another injury during a loss to the Portland Trail Blazers on February 27th, 2015. With the Thunder behind in the dying seconds, Russell attempted to purposely miss his free throw so the team could grab the offensive rebound and possibly tie the score with a follow-up. However, Russell was knocked to the ground as he followed his shot.

The fallen guard accidentally took a knee in the face courtesy of teammate Andre Roberson who was rushing to foul a Blazer and stop the clock. Russell, obviously in pain, later stood up, brushed it aside and finished the game. The sequence would become legendary to Westbrook fans, as Russell stayed in and finished the game with a literal dent in his face, on his cheekbone. He later had surgery to repair the zygoma fracture on his right cheek.

Russell finished the regular season with only 67 games played. However, the numbers he put up during those games were phenomenal. In fact, his 28.1 point scoring average won him his first scoring crown. He was in a tight race with former teammate, James Harden, for the scoring championship but a 37-point explosion in his last game, a win against the Timberwolves, pushed him past "The Beard", who finished with a 27.4 PPG average. Russell's 23 first quarter points and 34 first half points in his scoring title-clinching game were franchise records as well.

Russell was not that happy with his achievement as the win was not enough to take the Thunder to the playoffs. Ever the warrior, Russell said he preferred to still be playing and chasing after the championship rather than sitting at home watching the playoffs with the scoring title under his belt.

Eighth Season (2015-16)

In 80 games, Russell compiled career-highs in assists and rebounds while scoring 23.5 points per game, good for 8th place. His 7.8 rebound average put him at 30th place overall, highest for a guard, along with big men Zach Randolph and Brook Lopez. He even out-rebounded taller players such as Carmelo Anthony, LeBron James and Al Horford. His 481 defensive rebounds was the 18th highest for the year.

He grabbed 19 rebounds in a victory over Orlando on February 3rd. That figure put him in the sixth spot on the list of guards (fifth among point guards) with the most rebounds in a game. The highest total is 22 rebounds by former Nugget Lafayette "Fat" Lever. Fat also has the second, fourth, and fifth most rebounds among guards. Russell's 17 rebounds in a 2013 game ranks 15th in the list.

Russell continued his growth as a facilitator, as he ranked second in assists behind Sacramento's Rajon Rondo, with an average of 10.4 APG. Russell has always been a defensive demon and his 163 total steals and 2.0 steals per game average (fifth overall) proved just that.

Ninth Season (2016-17)

The offseason has been a tumultuous one for the City of Oklahoma. They just lost the face of the franchise after KD signed with the Golden State Warriors as he continues his quest for the Larry O'Brien Championship Trophy. Defensive specialist Serge Ibaka will also wear a new uniform when the 2016-17 season unfolds, as he was traded to the Orlando Magic in an effort to get younger and free more of the team's salary cap to keep Durant.

While they lost out on KD, the team did get a potential star in Victor Oladipo and a serviceable stretch four in Ersan Ilyasova. Lithuanian rookie Domantas Sabonis also arrives from the Magic and is expected to benefit from his stint in the Rio Olympics. With Ibaka gone, Steven Adams, Enes Kanter, Ilyasova and Sabonis will now handle the shaded lane. Veteran Nick Collison and Mitch McGary will still be there to provide spot minutes.

The team also let go of Dion Waiters, DJ Augustin and Randy Foye, opening up more playing time for Oladipo, Cameron Payne, and Anthony Morrow. The small forward position is also up for grabs and the likely candidates are

70-game starter Andre Roberson, Spaniard Olympian Alex Abrines, Kyle Singler, and Josh Huestis.

Aside from losing Durant, the biggest news of the Thunder offseason is the contract extension signed by Westbrook. The new three-year, $85 million agreement locks Russell up until the 2018 season, while he has the option to opt out in 2019. At the end of his contract, Russell will be eligible for a max contract starting at 35 % of the cap. Clearly, Russell is the biggest winner here. He's now the main star of the Thunder and he'll soon be paid like one. While the team may have its growing pains with all the newcomers, Russell will certainly make sure that they keep their winning ways.

What lies beyond 2018 is anybody's guess, though Russell has said time and again that he's committed to Oklahoma City as he "knows where he wants to be". One thing's for sure, though, his contact extension paved the way for the Thunder to acquire another All-Star talent. This early, Oklahoma native Blake Griffin rumors are rife. The LA Clippers star will become a free agent next year and his addition would certainly be huge for OKC.

Russell has also been the subject of rumors related to the Los Angeles Lakers. Many believe that the opportunity to come home to California would be the driving force of the Lakers' pitch as they vie for Russell's services. With the contract extension, they have lost out on getting him next season. However, that gives the Lakers at least a year to improve their roster and make it more palatable for stars such as Westbrook to come and play for the Purple and Gold.

Russell was one of the candidates for the US Men's Basketball Team that will defend the gold in the Rio Olympics. However, Russell declined the invitation, stating that he had a lengthy conversation with his family and they all agreed that passing up the opportunity this time around was for the best. Though Russell missed only a couple of games in the recently concluded season, the time off could help rest his body and prepare him for the upcoming one.

Chapter 4:

Personal Adult Life

Russell is certainly one of the most unique and interesting players in the entire National Basketball Association, and possibly even in all of the major American sports.

He is known for his fashion sense and was a fixture at the 2012 Fashion Week in New York as he leveraged his passion for fashion into a business opportunity. Russell launched his own clothing line, Westbrook XO with Barney's New York. His collection includes pieces that are very appealing to the young, hip crowd who often find Westbrook's confidence in trying new looks very appealing. Russell has even been considered a fashion icon, especially known for his post-game outfits.

However, Russell has style everywhere he goes and doesn't just dress up for his games. He can be seen sporting a variety of looks during the season or even in the off-season when he visits back home in Los Angeles. Oddly enough, most of Russell's fashion critics do not possess a notable sense of style and are clearly not the risky types, pretty much "armchair critics". He clearly has the respect of people within the industry, proven by his ability to work with Barney's and go to fashion shows with the likes of Anna Wintour.

Russell also works with the well-known sneaker giant, Jordan Brand. In late 2012, he signed a contract with Jordan Brand and has appeared in multiple commercials as an ambassador for the company.

Other endorsements include Kings and Jaxs Boxer Briefs, Subway, as well as many other companies that he believes in. It is fair to say that Russell is a very marketable player because of his light-hearted personality off the court combined with his intense persona on the court.

Also, Russell is a Christian and values family immensely. He has a younger brother, Raynard, and keeps a very close relationship with him. Russell's family has always supported him in his endeavors and he has been able to provide them with an amazing platform now that he has become successful.

Even though many star athletes say that their family means a lot to them, Russell truly means it. His father was integral in Russell's development, both as a man and as a basketball player. He would run dunes in Manhattan Beach with his younger brother Raynard. His mother can always be seen supporting Russell at his charitable events and serves as a major role model in Russell's life. Even as he has achieved such impressive stardom, Russell still spends a great deal of time with his family and enjoys just hanging out with his younger brother when he can.

On August 29th, 2015, Russell married his college sweetheart, Nina Ann-Marie Earl. Nina got game, too. Back in high school, she averaged 21.6 points, 6.7 rebounds, 3.1 assists, 3.8 steals, and 1.1 blocks as a senior at Diamond Ranch. The two-time CIF Player of the Year later enrolled at UCLA, where she was a part-time starter until she exhausted her playing years.

Chapter 5:

Philanthropic/Charitable Acts

Russell has been involved in a number of charitable events during his short time as a professional athlete. One of these includes an annual charity bowling event that he hosts. The "Why Not?" charity bowling event is held in Oklahoma City, raising money to benefit Russell's "Why Not? Foundation". A number of teammates, fellow NBA players, and other celebrities and influencers have attended the Annual Why Not? Bowl.

The foundation makes a big impact in the Oklahoma City community, providing opportunities for underprivileged students to access books that they would otherwise not be able to.

Russell is also an ambassador of sorts for reading. His foundation has even partnered with Scholastic and opened a reading room called "Russell's Reading Rooms". The reading room will help kids to develop a passion for learning through reading. It will also serve as a place for like-minded children to prosper, allowing them to avoid the pitfalls that many inner-city youth fall into.

During the 2014-15 season, his foundation succeeded in adding three more reading centers in Oklahoma City. Around 1,200 books were made available in three public schools where the students may come over and grab a book anytime they wish. Aside from books, the foundation also donates audio libraries and listening stations where children get to listen while learning. As of now, Russell has opened nine reading rooms and continues to buy books for the children. A book fair is held in these schools where Russel's Reading Rooms are. During the fair, each kid is provided with a certificate that allows them to choose and bring home a book for free.

As mentioned earlier, Russell was greatly impacted by the loss of his close friend, Khelcey Barrs. However, he went an extra step to help Khelcey's family as a youngster, when he decided to aid Barrs' grandmother in chores that Khelcey would normally partake in. This show of affection was very powerful for her and shows just how selfless Russell is.

Knowing the pain of losing a loved one, Russell has turned his attention to helping the Greater Than Aids campaign, which spreads awareness of the dreaded AIDS virus. He joined fellow NBA players Pau Gasol, Al Horford, and WNBA player Candice Wiggins, whose father passed away in 1991 due to AIDS, in a series of PSAs that talks about the dangers of the disease and the ways to help those who suffer from it. The Greater Than Aids campaign also visits communities, including in NBA arenas, to promote its message.

Along with the community involvement that the Why Not? Foundation provides, it also hosts a Youth Basketball Camp in Los Angeles. The camp is held at the Jesse Owens Recreation Center - the same center that Russell grew up playing basketball in at the age of seven. Russell not only teaches hands on basketball tips to the youngsters, but also imparts wisdom about life. He encourages them to believe in their own abilities just as he has, as well as to keep faith that they can overcome whatever challenges come their way.

In 2015, Russell made sure 850 children at the local Boys & Girls Club in Oklahoma City would have a great Thanksgiving Dinner. Russell, along with his wife and younger brother, all wearing "Why Not?" aprons, served the kids and their families a healthy serving of mashed potatoes and gravy to go with other Thanksgiving staples.

Russell has been sponsoring Thanksgiving Dinners for the impoverished for quite a while now. Aside from that, he also takes kids from Oklahoma and his hometown Los Angeles out to go shopping. He also often hosts parties during the holidays for more underprivileged families and homeless children like those at City Rescue Mission.

Russell has granted quite a number of wishes from the Make-A-Wish Foundation and has helped out in every way he can in other charitable events. He can be seen packing food for events and even serving them as he always does during Thanksgiving. He also finds time to visit children in hospitals and Thunder FIT clinics. For him and many other NBA ballers for that matter, children who suffer from various serious ailments deserve a break. A visit from someone like him is enough to lift up the spirits of the children for weeks, but he also makes sure to help them out in other ways.

Russell likes surprises. He once surprised a 19-year old mother of two young boys with a brand new car. Kerstin Gonzales was in a meeting at the Sunbeam Family Services office in Oklahoma City when Westbrook came from behind to tell her the good news. Gonzales got pregnant at the age of fourteen and again at sixteen. The young lady was forced to become an adult early on, but her hard work and persistence allowed her to finish high school while juggling work and taking care of her children.

Russell heard about her plight and with the help of Sunbeam, gamely gave her the Kia SUV he won for being the Most Valuable Player of the 2015 All-Star Game held in New York City. Gonzales usually borrowed a car from family or friends when she needed to take her kids somewhere. With the new car, things would be a lot easier for the young family.

Many find Russell's fashion sense quite surprising as well. Nevertheless, he leveraged his position as a fashion icon into charity. Russell has donated ties to the career Gear Celebrity Tie Auction. The objective of the auction is to help disadvantaged people, especially men, in getting jobs. Career Gear, a non-profit organization, arranges free workshops that teach how to apply and keep jobs. They also provide free wardrobe. Russell is not the only one to lend a hand. Fellow NBA stars Tyreke Evans, Carmelo Anthony and Dwyane Wade along with celebrities such as Kevin Bacon, Kevin Spacey, Gordon Ramsay, and Jay Leno have all donated ties to Career Gear.

Russell continues to help as much as he can through his foundation. He was rewarded for his charitable efforts with the season-long NBA Cares Community Assist Award back in the 2014-15 season. The award is given to an NBA player who best exemplifies the NBA's vision and passion for sharing their fortunes and giving back to the community. Because of this award, the league also donated $25,000 to Russell's foundation, which only added to the many ways Russell has helped Oklahomans and even those outside his adopted hometown.

Chapter 6:

Legacy, Potential & Inspiration

Russell's legacy is still being created and he is just starting to hit his prime. However, his polarizing personality and impactful presence is already being felt. Whether he is inspiring the youth and connecting with youngsters off the court, or fearlessly attacking seven footers in mid-air launches towards the rim, Russell has personality traits that are truly rare.

As an athlete, he keeps developing each year that he plays, evident in his abilities to thrive in the point guard role despite playing off-guard at UCLA. He continues to grow as a leader and teammate each and every day and is a key reason why the small-market Oklahoma City Thunder have achieved such great success in such a short period of time.

His passing is an underrated aspect of his game, as he always is one of the league leaders in assists per game. His average of almost seven assists per game for his career shows that he does a great job of creating opportunities for others on the court. As mentioned earlier, he is one of the best rebounding guards in the league and his defense as a point guard is among the best as well. This combination has put Russell into the conversation amongst the best all-around players in the game, with the likes of LeBron James, Kawhi Leonard, Paul George, and Chris Paul.

Russell still can improve his three point shooting, leadership, and decision making, but he has already come quite a long way from the "risky" pick that he was just a few years ago. He was a late bloomer that decided to believe in himself when only his family and friends gave him a shot. He carries the weight of his lost friend, the Westbrook name, and the passionate fanbase of the Thunder everywhere he goes.

One thing that is clearly missing in Russell's career is an awesome nickname. Many of the game's brightest are known by aliases. Of course, there's "Magic" whose nickname best exemplifies his flair and talent, while "His Airness" got his moniker for his gravity-defying moves. Among the current crop of NBA ballers, we have Durantula, King James, CP3, and the recently retired Black Mamba and the Big Fundamental.

Many have tried giving Russell a nickname but none so far have given him justice. He's been called "Fashion Icon" because of his outlandish style. Teammate Enes Kanter calls him "Beastbrook" which suits him because of his penchant to attack the rim like a beast.

The sickest moniker so far, thanks to the Jordan Brand, is none other than "WestWolf". During Super Bowl 50, fans were delighted to watch a TV spot featuring Westbrook and the newest shoe from the famed Jordan Brand. The Air Jordan XXX was introduced while Westbrook, clad in his OKC uniform, was making a grand entrance through a crowd and into the arena with "Blockbuster Night Part 1" by Run the Jewels blaring in the background. A teenaged kid is seen and heard blabbing about Westbrook not getting a triple double "since yesterday". The loud-mouthed youngster finishes off by calling the NBA star "Westwolf" and howling like a wolf.

Conclusion

Hopefully this book was able to help you gain inspiration from the life of Russell Westbrook, one of the best players currently playing in the National Basketball Association.

The rise and fall of a star is often the cause for much wonder. But most stars have an expiration date. In basketball, once a star player reaches his mid- to late-thirties, it is often time to contemplate retirement. What will be left in people's minds about that fading star? In Russell's case, people will remember how he led a franchise in their journey towards a championship. He will be remembered as the guy who plucked his franchise from obscurity, helped them build their image, and honed his own image along the way.

Russell has also inspired so many people because he is the star who never fails to connect with fans and give back to the less fortunate. Noted for his ability to impose his will on any game, he is a joy to watch on the basketball court. Last but not least, he's remarkable for remaining simple and firm with his principles in spite of his immense popularity.

Hopefully you learned some great things about Russell in this book and are able to apply some of the lessons that you've learned to your own life! Good luck in your own journey!

Made in the USA
Lexington, KY
27 October 2016